MW01242272

Beautiful Night, Beautiful Me

By
Devondra Banks

To fling my arms wide,

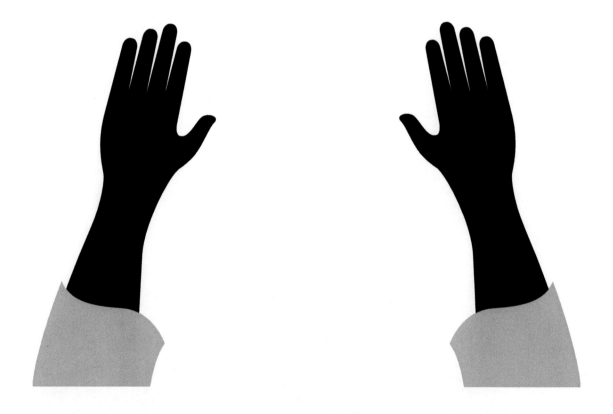

In some place of the sun,

To whirl
and to dance,

Till the white day is done.

Then rest at cool evening,

Beneath a tall tree,

While night comes on gently,

Dark like me,

That is my dream!

To fling my arms wide,

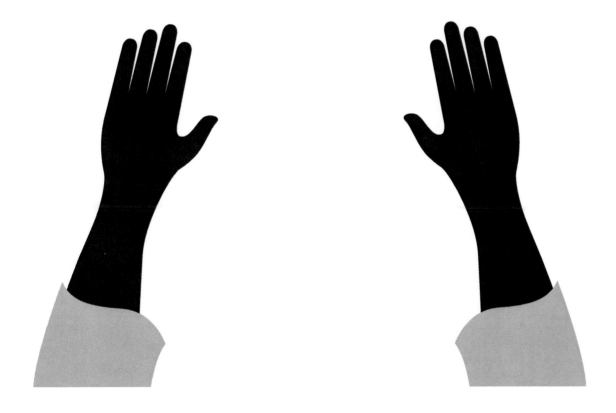

In the face of the sun,

Dance! Whirl! Whirl!

Till the quick day is done,

Rest at pale evening...

A tall, slim tree...

Night coming tenderly,

Black like me!